Jo Foster has been fascinated by history since she discovered that life hadn't always been like it was in 1980s Essex. Since studying history at university, she has made a living working in TV, researching programmes including *The Worst Jobs in History*, *Time Team* and *Who Do You Think You Are?*

Jo lives in an old house in east London with her three housemates, and still wants to be a history spy when she grows up.

If I was a kid with a time machine, I'd want Jo Foster to be my guide. She has an insatiable historical curiosity, treats both the past and the present with verve and gusto and has a mischievous sense of humour that would keep me smiling throughout my journey.

Tony Robinson

ESCAPE FROM VESUVIUS

HISTORY SPIES

JO FOSTER

ILLUSTRATED BY SCOULAR ANDERSON

MACMILLAN CHILDREN'S BOOKS

First published 2009 by Macmillan Children's Books
a division of Macmillan Publishers Limited
20 New Wharf Road, London N1 9RR
Basingstoke and Oxford
Associated companies throughout the world
www.panmacmillan.com

ISBN 978-0-330-44900-7

3 5 7 9 8 6 4

A CIP catalogue record for this book is available from the British Library.

Typeset by Perfect Bound Ltd
Printed and bound in the UK by CPI Mackays, Chatham ME5 8TD

To my parents

Once upon a time, my life was almost as boring as yours.

Then on my birthday last year I got a phone call; it was a bloke from the Department for Historical Accuracy. See, the government had invented a way to go back in time. They wanted someone to travel around and check up on what really happened in history. And they picked me. Probably because of my astounding talents and unusually large brain, I expect.

Since then I've been travelling through time, spying on the craziest stuff. Battles and magicians and feasts and duels. All sorts!

And now you're coming along too, and you're with the best guide around. I'll make sure you get to see everything that's worth seeing!

I'll show you what to wear, what to eat, where to go, how people have fun, where they live – everything. Stick with me and almost nothing can go wrong.

Department for Historical Accuracy

HISTORY SPY 00001

NAME CHARLIE CARTWRIGHT

CLEARANCE ULTRA

Pass must be carried at all times when on official missions. Not valid without stamp.

Our next top-secret History Spy mission is to...

POMPEII AD 79

If you want to be a History Spy you have to learn to be invisible. It's not magic – the best way to be invisible is to look just like everyone else.

Like in our time, if you just start doing the flamenco in the high street, people are going to stare.

You have to pick the right place.

Here you can share my extremely confidential History Spies' Fact File. It's all important stuff cos it'll help you go unnoticed. And that could save your life.

OK. First of all we're getting you into some proper clothes. I mean, look at us – we'll look ridiculous like this!

MISSION MAKEOVER

You'd think it'd be simple to dress up as a Roman, right? Just wrap a sheet round yourself and there's your toga. Well, you'd be wrong. Unless you want to blow our cover and get us both in trouble, you need to learn a few rules for getting dressed.

Tunic – the safest choice. Most people wear one of these most of the time, so you can get away with it wherever you are. It's like a long T-shirt, usually made of wool or linen.

You can look almost right by borrowing a grown-up's baggy T-shirt and tying a bit of string round your waist. It's a bit draughty, but it'll be fine once we get to sunny Italy.

White toga – it's the Roman costume everyone's heard of, but be careful. Only VIPs are allowed to wear it.

Plus, togas are a right hassle to get in and out of! You need a slave to help you put one on properly. You wouldn't bother unless you really wanted to show off.

White toga with purple edging – this is one step up, and just for the most important bigwigs. Only certain kinds of rich men get to wear these.

Stola – a dress for married women. Basically just a longer, fancier tunic.

Palla – a colourful shawl to be worn on top of the stola when going out. Female History Spies can drape a palla over their heads so as not to be recognized. This feature is also useful if you get caught in the rain.

Paenula – hooded poncho for cold or wet weather.

> Look, a Roman hoodie! Ha, best keep out of **his** way!

TO DYE OR NOT TO DYE?

It might seem like everyone wears pretty much the same thing in Roman times – tunics, and the occasional extra sheet. But people will get *most* annoyed if you wear the wrong colour. Only rich people wear bright colours, and there's one colour you should be extremely careful with: purple. Purple dye is ridiculously expensive because it only comes from a special kind of shellfish called a **murex**. You need about 10,000 murex to dye just one toga!

So the more purple you see someone wearing, the more powerful they are – and the more they smell of old shellfish.

HERE'S A HANDY KEY

Narrow band of purple: equites

Could definitely get you beaten up.

Broad band of purple: senators

Could get you sent to work in the mines.

Loads of purple, a laurel wreath and plenty of bodyguards: the Emperor!

Could get you beaten up, sent to work in the mines and then thrown to the lions.

THE FINISHING TOUCHES

Sandals: The *only* footwear to be seen in this year. Remember, there are very few times in history when it's acceptable to wear socks with sandals – and this isn't one of them.

Faceache: Without soap, decent razors or proper mirrors, shaving can cut your face to bits. If this happens to you, reach for a Roman-style plaster – a spider's web soaked in oil and vinegar. Try to make sure no spiders are still attached. Shaving's such a pain that some men get their beards plucked out with tweezers instead.

Hairdos: Men should keep their hair short, though if you want to look trendy you could get your slave to curl it and put oil in it as well. Rich ladies can really go to town, with huge wigs, sky-high hairdos and silver combs for added sparkle. The hair in wigs comes from slaves, of course, or you can buy silky blonde hair from German prisoners, shiny black hair all the way from India, or even curly ginger hair from Britain. Some women spend all morning getting dolled up.

MAKE YOUR OWN MAKE-UP

If you want to try painting your face like a Roman lady, you'll need a strong stomach and the following ingredients:

Soot scraped from an old lamp: to paint your eyebrows and eyelashes black

Ash and goat fat: to dye your hair blonde

Ash from the fire: for eyeshadow

Bird droppings: a great remedy for pimples

Poisonous white lead powder: to make your face look as if it's never seen the sun

Sludge from the bottom of a wine barrel: to make your cheeks and lips red

Well, these clothes smell pretty ancient, at least! We'll fit right in.

One last check, just in case:

- **NO trousers!** If you wear trousers people will think you're a savage barbarian from Britain or somewhere else where the people don't know how to act like Romans. And that's not the look we're going for right now.

- **NO watches!** The Romans use sundials, hourglasses and water clocks to tell the time. And you can't carry any of those around on your wrist.

- **NO buttons!** Hold your clothes together with a brooch instead.

- **NO glasses!** They won't be invented for about another 1,200 years. Keep a sharp-eyed slave handy if your eyesight's not great.

We're not supposed to be here, remember. The Romans can get pretty nasty if they don't like someone. I mean, some of the emperors get pretty nasty with their own families! So seriously – try to keep out of real trouble.
Don't forget, it's not just about how you look. If we remember this important stuff we should be fine.

POMPEII: VITAL BACKGROUND BRIEFING

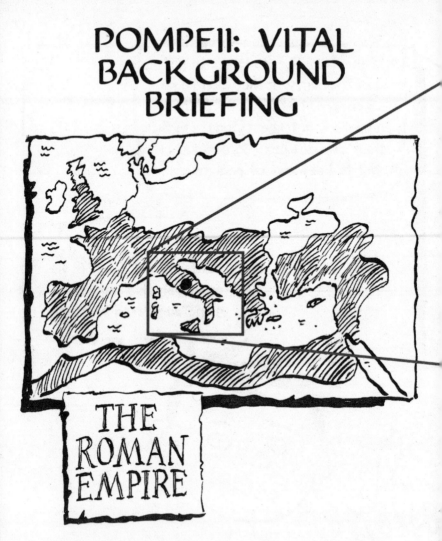

THE ROMAN EMPIRE

Population: About 10,000 (actually, we're not sure – any more information History Spies can find about this would be very useful).

Location: Pompeii is an important port on the Sarnus River in the south of the Roman province of Italia.

Agents should find it easy to find their way around Pompeii. The town is built on a grid pattern, with straight roads between blocks of houses called **insulae**. Remember there aren't any street names or house numbers, though.

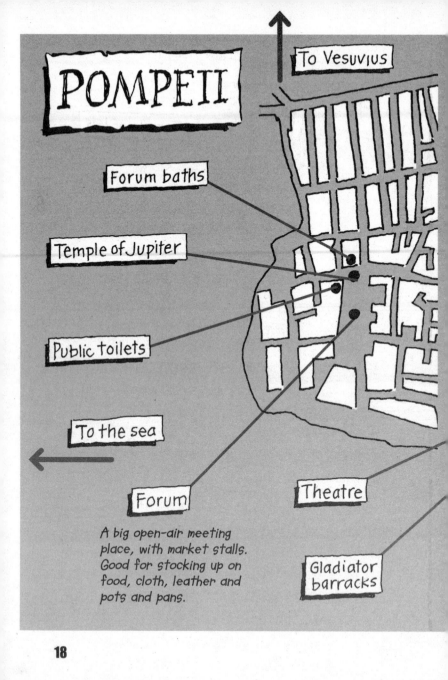

POMPEII

To Vesuvius

Forum baths

Temple of Jupiter

Public toilets

To the sea

Forum

A big open-air meeting place, with market stalls. Good for stocking up on food, cloth, leather and pots and pans.

Theatre

Gladiator barracks

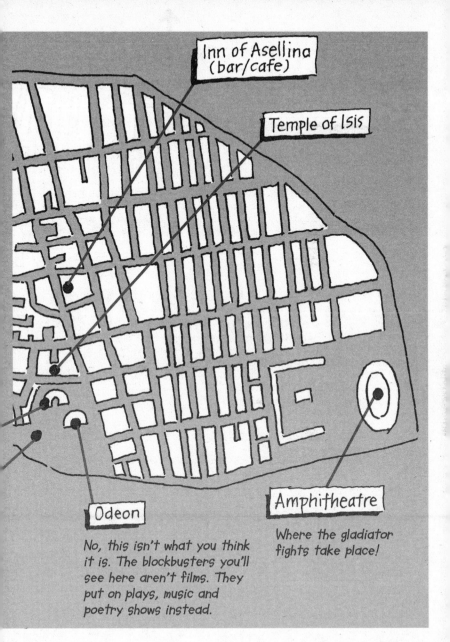

Inn of Asellina
(bar/cafe)

Temple of Isis

Odeon

No, this isn't what you think
it is. The blockbusters you'll
see here aren't films. They
put on plays, music and
poetry shows instead.

Amphitheatre

Where the gladiator
fights take place!

GETTING AROUND

Transport options are limited in Ancient Roman times. There are no cars, trains, planes, buses, or even bikes.

> Even a scooter or a skateboard would be handy, but there's just so much stuff the Romans haven't invented yet. We may have to do some **exercise**.

AROUND TOWN

ON FOOT – the good news is that Pompeii is a small town. You can walk everywhere you need to go if you're staying inside the town walls.

LITTERS – a great way to travel for the rich. A litter is a covered seat that is carried around town. Litters keep

> I love these. Nothing says 'I'm dead important' like being carried around all day by slaves!

your feet free of street filth and keep the rain and sun off you too. You'll need four sturdy slaves to carry the poles – make sure they're all the same height and don't limp or you'll be in for a bumpy ride.

HORSE – if you're dressed as a wealthy person, you could ride a horse if you're in a hurry. There are special poles in the pavements so you can tie up your horse securely.

CART – carts go around the city carrying food, drink, rubbish, building materials and stuff for sale. History Spies can sometimes find it useful to hide in the back of a cart to travel around unseen.

ACROSS COUNTRY

BOAT – head for the river or the sea if you want to get out of Pompeii unnoticed. It's a busy port, and there are boats coming and going in all directions – along the river, up the coast to Rome, and even from as far away as Egypt.

CISIUM – the Roman version of a taxi. A cisium is a light chariot pulled by a mule. You can arrange a trip at the taxi stands outside the city gates.

WHERE TO STAY

ROOM AT THE INN

Inns have a bad reputation for being dirty and smoky (from the fires – no one smokes yet because there's no tobacco until someone discovers America). Thieves hang around inns too, so keep any valuables well hidden. Roman inns also have a reputation for bad food.

There's this story going round about a man who ate dinner in an inn and was drugged by the innkeeper's wife. Apparently she magically turned him into a horse and made him work for her every night! I think we'll get a snack from a food stall, just to be on the safe side.

TRAVEL MONEY

The English words 'money' and 'mint' are more glamorous than you'd think – they come from the name of a Roman goddess. Juno Moneta's temple was the first place where Roman coins were made. If you're travelling to Pompeii with a large amount of cash, you should take it to a temple. There aren't any banks, but the priests will look after your valuables.

Memorize the names of the most common coins so you'll know what to pick out when you pay for things.

copper: *as*

brass: *sestertius* (4 asses)

silver: *denarius* (4 sestertii)

gold: *aureus* (25 denarii)

You'll need your copper coins for small change. For instance, it costs half an *as* to go to the baths, or to buy a bit of bread for lunch.

If you want to be able to read the prices, you'll have to learn how the numbers (called Roman numerals) work. Their letters are the same as ours, but their numbers don't make nearly as much sense. Here are the numbers from 1 to 10:

So 4 is IV because it's one less than 5... but 6 is VI because it's one more than 5. I think I get it so far.

To go higher than 10 you'll need these numbers too:

L = 50

C = 100

D = 500

Φ / M = 1,000

Q = 500,000

Here are some bigger numbers, just to show you how it works:

LXXXIV = 84

MM = 2000

MMI = 2001

MCM = 1900

MCMLXXII = 1972

To test yourself, answer these questions in Roman numerals:

1. How many words are there in this sentence?
2. What year are you travelling back to for your mission to Pompeii?
3. How old are you?
4. What is James Bond's code number?

ANSWERS: 1: VIII 2: LXXIX 3: You should know! 4: Trick question – there's no 0 in Latin, 'VII' is as close as you'd get.

LOST IN TRANSLATION

Agents deployed to AD 79 should go on an intensive Latin course first.

Don't worry, it's fine – you're with me, I'll do the talking. Anyway Latin's easy. Loads of words are just like English.

See if you can guess what these mean:

MUSICA   VERSUS
SCHOLA   THEATRUM
POETICA   COLOR   NUMERUS

Reading should be easy because Romans use the same letters as we do.

ANSWERS: musica = music, versus = against, schola = school, theatrum = theatre, poetica = poetry, color = colour, numerus = number.

You may already have heard of some of these other Latin words and phrases:

ET CETERA – and the rest

VICE VERSA – the order reversed or swapped

VENI, VIDI, VICI – I came, I saw, I conquered (this is what Julius Caesar said when he'd won a great battle)

POST MORTEM – after death

Here are some of the important words you'll need:

ARA – altar for making sacrifices to the gods

ASTRAGALI – a game like jacks but played with bones (see p 70)

AUGUSTALES – priests who honour the emperors' memories

AVE – hello

CAUPONA – inn, lodging house

CAVE CANEM – beware of the dog

CENA – dinner, the main meal

CIVIS – a Roman citizen, a free person with the right to vote

CLIENS – inhabitant with limited rights who serves a patron

CONVIVIUM – dinner party

DECURIONS – members of the town's Senate. The guys in charge.

DIES NEFASTI – unlucky days in the calendar. Don't bother doing any work today – nobody else will.

DUUMVIRI – the most important magistrates. Two are elected every year to run the town.

FORUM – square in the centre of town where all the important deals are done

GARUM – fish-innards sauce

IENTACULUM – breakfast

PLEBEIAN – a common person, but still a citizen

PRANDIUM – lunch

SALVE – hi / how's it going? / bye

SENATE – law-making assembly in Rome

STOLA – woman's dress

STRIGIL – scraping stick to clean yourself with in the baths

THERMOPOLIUM – bar-cafe, handy for a quick snack

TOGA – the Roman version of a suit, for important men only

TRICLINIUM – dining room

VALE – goodbye

People still learn Latin today because it stayed so important in Europe. Even after Roman times all the clever, rich and important people used it for making laws and running the Church. You'll find it useful for spying missions to all kinds of other times and places.

WHAT YEAR IS IT AGAIN?

To get to Pompeii, you set the annostat to AD 79, because that's how we count years now. AD stands for 'Anno Domini' (the year of our Lord), meaning it's 79 years since Jesus Christ was born. But in Pompeii, they don't think it's AD 79 at all. Most Romans round here haven't even heard of Jesus yet. Instead, they name the year after whichever two consuls are in charge of Rome at the time. It works because the consuls swap around every year, but if you don't keep up with the news, you won't know what year it is.

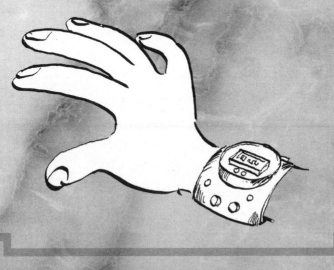

WHAT KIND OF PERSON ARE YOU?

The people who 'count' in Pompeii are the citizens. They can vote and own their own stuff, and they're protected by the law. Make sure you dress and act appropriately for the kind of person you're supposed to be.

Patricians

PATRICIANS: the richest, most respected people. As a patrician, you own lots of land and run the law and the army. Act as snooty as you like.

EQUITES: rich businessmen. You can make sure everyone knows just how rich you are by having wild parties and huge houses. You do have to do some business too, though.

Equites

PLEBEIANS: ordinary people. You might be a farmer, a trader or a shopkeeper. Let's face it, you're nothing special.

But all these people are citizens and they have much better lives than slaves.

SLAVES aren't citizens and they have no rights at all. Once you're bought by someone, you belong completely to them.

IT'S WEIRD AT THE TOP

The Emperor usually stays in Rome, and a good thing too as far as Pompeii's concerned. Emperors are dangerous to have around, because they're so powerful. Everyone worships them – literally! There are temples all over the place to dead emperors. When they die, they go up to heaven. Just to make sure everyone believes that little story, when a dead emperor is burned at his funeral, someone will sneakily release an eagle at the same time so everyone can see his 'soul' fly away.

> You definitely wouldn't want to work for any of these guys, but some emperors are hilarious!

JULIUS CAESAR: murdered by Brutus, Cassius and a bunch of others when he got too big for his boots. Not actually an emperor – he was a dictator.

OCTAVIAN: defeated Cleopatra and got Egypt into the Roman Empire. Caesar's adopted son. Became the first ever Roman Emperor in 27 BC.

DOMITIAN: made everyone call him 'Lord and God'.

CLAUDIUS: his son Drusus had an embarrassing end. He was larking around and threw a pear in the air and caught it in his mouth. Unluckily, it got stuck in his throat and he choked to death.

CALIGULA: 'Caligula' means 'little boot'. His real name was Gaius, but he got his nickname because of the shoes he wore when he was a kid. He was cruel, and probably mad. Tried to get his horse a top job in government. Murdered by his own guards.

35

NERO: played the lyre and fancied himself as a rock star. May have started a massive fire in Rome on purpose because he was bored and wanted a new city. Blamed the fire on the Christians. Played in the Olympic Games and fixed it so he won every event. He had his own mother murdered, killed his wife and then killed himself.

GALBA, OTHO, VITELLIUS AND VESPASIAN:

AD 69 was known as 'the year of the four emperors', because all these men had a turn at being emperor – but never for very long. Vespasian won out in the end, and he kept his job for ten more years. Vespasian was pretty good, and he either had a sense of humour or a giant ego. When he died in AD 79, he said, 'Damn it, I think I'm becoming a god!'

TITUS: Vespasian's son. He's young and handsome, and seems to be doing OK – but then he's only been in the job a couple of months. In AD 81 he'll die, and there are rumours it's a poisoning. Being Emperor is a risky job.

CODENAME: CORNELIUS

Remember to call me Cornelius when we're here. It sounds more Roman than Charlie!

History Spies should use codenames when you're working in a place where your own name would stand out as foreign or unusual.

Romans usually have three names. Here's the full name that Agent Charlie Cartwright has chosen:

Gaius Cornelius Rufus

Gaius comes first because it's his **praenomen** – only his family would use that at home. There aren't very many praenomens to choose from. Try picking one from this list:

Appius   Decimus   Lucius

Marcus   Numerius   Publius

Quintus   Sextus   Tiberius   Vibius

Cornelius is Charlie's **nomen** – the name he'll use most often, and also the name people get from their fathers. It's a bit like your surname.

Here are some other nomens you'll hear in Pompeii:

Calpurnius   Claudius   Cuspius

Fabius   Flavius   Julius

Lucretius   Livineius

Poppaeus   Popidius

Romanus   Satrius   Vettius

Rufus is Charlie's **cognomen**, which is like a nickname.

I wanted to be Rufus because it means 'red' and that's my favourite colour, but you can pick another one to suit you:

Ampliatus   *Polybius*   Verus

Eros   Felix (this one means 'happy')

Secundus   *Valens*   Severus   *Britannicus*

These are all men's names – to make them into women's names, wherever there's an 'us' at the end, just change it to an 'a'. A girl called Claudia probably has a father called Claudius. Women and girls often have only two names rather than three, and really unimportant people like slaves only have one name.

OK, enough of the briefing bit – it's time to go and spy on some real, live Ancient Romans!

39

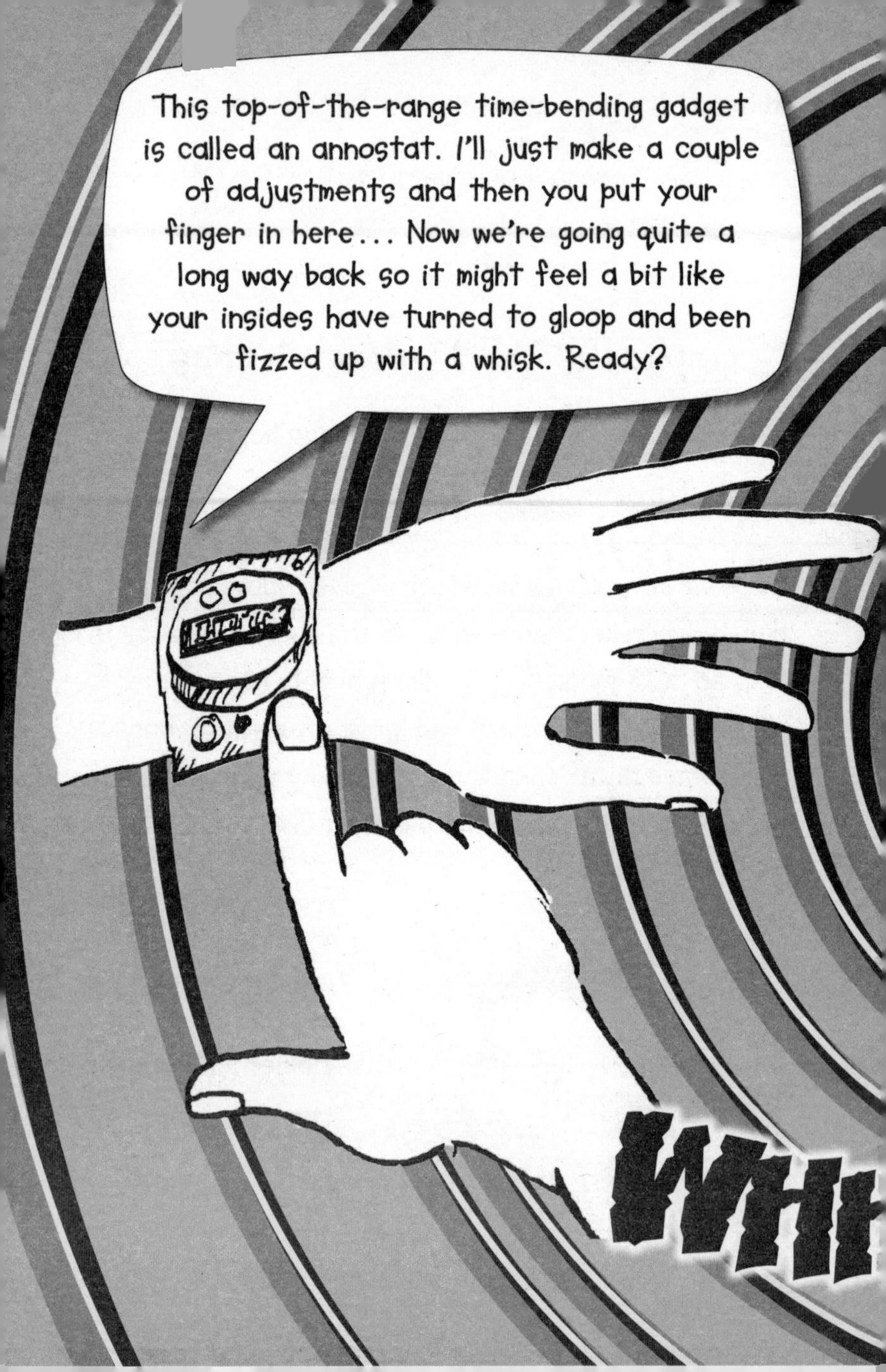
This top-of-the-range time-bending gadget is called an annostat. I'll just make a couple of adjustments and then you put your finger in here... Now we're going quite a long way back so it might feel a bit like your insides have turned to gloop and been fizzed up with a whisk. Ready?
WH

Ha! Works every time! Isn't this amazing?

We're in the Roman Empire! This is the Number One civilization in the world right now. They're in charge of everything. The Romans have it all – big cities, sunshine, a fantastic army, lots of impressive buildings, and slaves to do everything for them. The Empire stretches all the way to Britain, Morocco, Spain, Turkey... and here in Pompeii we're fairly close to the centre of it all.

If you've heard of this town it's probably because of that mountain over there. It's called Vesuvius. It may look green and pretty, but don't be fooled – it's an active volcano and any day now it's going to erupt. This whole place is going to be wiped out and no one knows it's coming except us. We've turned up just at the right time – or the wrong time, depending on how you look at it. Don't worry though – I've got a plan. I'll make sure we see all the action without getting hurt.

Because Pompeii was covered up so suddenly, archaeologists know loads about what it was like. But they're still arguing about what the stuff they've dug up means, so it's our job to help them work out exactly what's going on. So come on, let's go and explore while the city's still standing!

This is one of the main ways into the city – the Salt Gate. We'll head in this way and see what's going on.

Noisy, isn't it? I SAID... Oh, never mind.

NEED TO KNOW: HARD OF HEARING

History Spies who need to use listening devices (or 'bugs') in ancient Pompeii should be fully trained in how to avoid background noise. You'll have to contend with the usual noises of any ancient city.

'Factory' noise from workshops at the back of every shop: beating metal, smashing up marble and sawing wood

It gets worse. Pompeii's special noise pollution problem is that the whole city is a building site. Seventeen years ago there was a huge earthquake here, which destroyed many buildings and damaged almost everything. This was great news for builders who've been working non-stop ever since – and making a colossal hammering and banging noise.

Even the walls are noisy. There's graffiti everywhere. Maybe it's OK to write on the walls round here? I would love to give it a go – but the Department of Historical Accuracy would definitely think that was changing history. If they found out they'd take my annostat away and I'd be grounded in the twenty-first century forever. Ugh.

TALKING WALLS

Keep a note of graffiti you see when you're walking around Pompeii. It can be useful because it tells us what people were thinking, and it's the kind of thing that doesn't get written down in other places.

From this wall, it looks like everyone's obsessed with getting elected and watching actors and sports stars. Doesn't change much, does it?

ROADS, AND OTHER SCIENTIFIC WONDERS

Roman roads are famous, and they'll still be famous in two thousand years' time. They're just one example of the amazing level of Roman engineering. Romans build roads better than anyone else, with three layers: first, concrete and broken stones; then coarse sand and lime; and on top, blocks of stone set in concrete, packed with flint and pebbles. Plus the roads curve downward at the edges, so when it rains the water runs off instead of making puddles.

You definitely want to stick to the pavement round here. See how the street's so much lower? And those big stone blocks in the middle of the road over there – they're stepping stones so you can cross the road without losing your sandal in all the muck! There are all sorts down there: donkey poo, people pee, rotting vegetable peelings, dead cats...

This is what it looks like now

The Romans have worked out how to build all kinds of impressive and useful things. They're fantastic at using arches, which makes their bridges incredibly strong. They also use arches for **aqueducts** – bridges that carry water across them, so that whole towns can get supplies of clean drinking water.

And then they have great plumbing, so the water can go all around the city to people's houses.

They have clocks too – sundials and water clocks mean that Romans can tell the time instead of just knowing when it gets light and dark. The great thing is, in the summer when the days are longer, so are the hours! In winter a daytime hour is about forty-five minutes, and in summer it's more like an hour and a quarter.

So in winter, a school day would be... five hours instead of six and a half! Do you think we could bring that back?

Some Romans invent so many gadgets that they don't know what to use them all for. Hero of Alexandria is a great scientist who lives in Egypt. He's invented all kinds of things, from a whistling bird powered by water to the steam engine. When people next start playing with the steam engine, more than 1,500 years later, it changes the world. They use it to power trains, spin cotton and shape metal. But Hero just invents it, shows it off to his friends, who think it's pretty, and never works out how useful it could be.

WHISTLING BIRD
POWERED BY
WATER
BY HERO OF ALEXANDRIA

51

> This is the Forum. This is where all the big business deals are done. We've come straight to the centre of the city.

SHOP, WORK AND PRAY – IN ONE HANDY SQUARE

The Forum is an important place in any Roman town. To find information about who's doing well, who has gone bankrupt and which ships have just come in from where, agents should come here in the morning to listen in on all the business deals being made.

The Macellum is a covered market in the Forum where you can buy raw meat and fish, if you've got somewhere to cook it. Also in the Forum you'll find stalls selling general bits and bobs, especially on Saturdays – Pompeii's big market day. The basilica is here too (the hall where the magistrates meet and where they try criminals) as well as the temples of Jupiter, Apollo, the Emperor, and the city's own gods.

The Forum is also where you can find out most of the big news from all over the Empire – it'll be stuck on a wall, and everyone will be talking about the latest wars and gossip from Rome.

THE DAILY EMPIRE

THE FROZEN NORTH

OUT IN BRITAIN GENERAL GNAEUS JULIUS AGRICOLA IS BRINGING CIVILIZATION TO THE BRITISH BARBARIAN BRUTES. HE'S TRYING TO MAKE THEM HAVE BATHS AND STOP WEARING TROUSERS.

NEWS HEADLINES

BONG! – IT'S COLOSSAL!

In Rome, the new Emperor Titus is building an amphitheatre called the Colosseum, set to open next year. Sources close to the Emperor say it's going to be bigger and better than any other amphitheatre. Of course, everyone in Pompeii knows they're just copying ours.

BONG! – THE FROZEN NORTH

Out in Britain, General Gnaeus Julius Agricola is bringing civilization to the British barbarian brutes. He's trying to make them have baths and stop wearing trousers .

There's definitely something exciting going on this morning. Look at all these people in their best togas. They've even dressed up that pig in a ribbon and some pretty flowers... Oh! Tell you what, if you're a sensitive vegetarian I think you should look away now.

HOLIDAY TIME ~ LET'S KILL SOMETHING!

Romans kill a lot of animals to keep their gods happy. They dress up an animal and bring it to the front of a temple where a priest says a prayer over it – and then a burly man with a sledgehammer hits it on the head, and they stab it to death. Later on, they'll burn the best bits of the sacrificed animal for the gods. Then the rest of it gets cooked and eaten by everyone else.

> Hmm... I wonder how long we have to wait around for the holy hog roast?

Pigs are the favourite 'food' of the god Augustus. It's his festival at the end of August.

There are plenty of other festivals to see, whichever time of year you visit Pompeii, including:

- The birthday of the god **MARS** (1 March) – the parties go on for several weeks.

- **PROCESSION OF THE BOAT** (5 March) – the statue of the goddess Isis gets brought out of her temple in Pompeii and taken down to the sea. A favourite festival for sailors.
- **SATURNALIA** (17 December) – festival of the god Saturn. People eat too much, give each other presents, and generally go wild. There won't be any such thing as Christmas for another few hundred years, but Saturnalia is a lot like it.

They get everywhere, Roman gods. There are statues of them on the street corners, in cupboards in the house, even in the loo... and there are so many of them!

Romans worship different gods in different places and on different days. One way is to pick your favourite god or goddess, head to their temple, pour a bit of wine or olive oil on the ground by their statue and wait for results. When you're on a mission in Roman times you should remember to do this regularly. Romans don't trust people who don't worship their gods. In fact, you should worship as many gods as you can as often as you can.

PICK A GOD, ANY GOD...

Got a specific problem and need divine assistance? Maybe one of this lot can help.

JUPITER – King of the gods. Controls thunder, lightning, rain and storms. Also looks after bakers.

JUNO – Jupiter's wife and top goddess. In charge of childbirth, marriage and the moon. Hangs out with a peacock and holds a sceptre. The month of June is named after her.

MINERVA – a warrior-goddess. Looks after education, doctors, musicians and craftsmen.

MARS – the war god, and also the god of fields. His month is March, when his festival is celebrated, and in some languages he gets Tuesday named after him (it's Mardi in French).

DIANA – goddess of the moon, hunting and wild beasts.

MERCURY – the messenger god and god of trade. Wears a winged hat and winged shoes and is mates with a cockerel, a goat and a tortoise.

VENUS – the goddess of love. You can see her all over Pompeii, on shop signs and in people's houses. She protects sailors.

VULCAN – an ugly god. He's a blacksmith who lives inside a volcano, heating up his forge and banging bits of metal together. Metalworkers worship him.

Maybe people in Pompeii should be paying him more attention right now – after all, the volcano's about to get very, very angry.

BACCHUS – god of wine. Handy if you're having a party.

ISIS – an Egyptian goddess who's really popular in Pompeii right now, especially with rich people. Pompeii is on the way by boat from Egypt to north Italy, so there's Egyptian stuff all over the place. Isis protects sailors. She also offers life after death as a special bonus gift, which most of the other gods haven't thought of.

MITHRAS – a god for soldiers. Mithras is a Persian god who's worshipped in a secret cult all over the Empire. He's no use to women because they're not allowed in his gang.

I've heard a rumour that when you sign up for this religion, you have to lie in a pit while people kill a bull and pour the blood all over you!

SECRETS OF THE MYSTERY GODS

The cults of Isis and Mithras are both called 'mystery religions' by historians. No one's allowed into their temples unless they're paid-up members, and they have secret rituals which no one else is allowed to know about. After an experienced History Spy has made several successful trips to Ancient Roman times, the Department is likely to send him or her on a mission to investigate one of these cults, to find out more about their secrets.

I would love to sneak a look inside the Temple of Isis. Apparently they have a whole load of secret holy treasures locked up in there!

JESUS CHRIST – There aren't that many Christians in the Roman Empire yet, and no one really trusts them. After the big fire in Rome fifteen years ago, the Emperor Nero blamed it on Christians and had some of them burned alive. If you want to stay out of trouble in Pompeii, it's best not to say you're a Christian.

STERCULINUS – the god of manure-spreading.

ROBIGUS – the god of mildew.

CARDEA – the goddess of door hinges.

Oh, now don't be ridiculous. These HAVE to be made up!

(They're not.)

Oh, Cardea, goddess of the door hinge, please protect my house and family!

SPYING ON THE FUTURE

The Romans have several daft ways to look into the future. History Spies, of course, can easily pretend to be expert fortune tellers because they can just travel forward and find out exactly what happens next.

Thing is, we're not allowed to tell people about really important things like the volcano erupting. That would count as changing history and it's totally against the rules.

If you plan to disguise yourself as a fortune teller, learn these Roman methods so you can tell everyone how you *really* know the future.

INNARDS: a **haruspex** is someone who roots around inside sacrificed animals to read signs of the future. The word haruspex means 'gut-gazer'!

This is the bit of the sacrifice that gets really messy. After they've killed the pig, they cut it open and have a look at all the guts and gloop inside. This guy's a fortune-teller, and he reckons you can see the future in the shape of a pig's liver. And you thought reading tea leaves was silly!

BIRDS: Augurs are priests who spend a lot of time looking at birds. They see the future in the way wild birds fly together, or whether a chicken eats its dinner. Augurs often go to war with the army to look after the sacred chickens who know whether a battle's going to go well or not.

LIGHTNING: a person called a **fulgurator** sees mystical signs in the amount of lightning there is in a storm, what shapes it makes, and where it strikes.

STARS: Romans are so daft they even believe you can see your future if you know which star sign you are.

Wow – it just goes to show, not all of the Romans' silly ideas have gone out of fashion. Horoscopes are still around in our time.

I think I've just had a vision of the future myself, and it's quite smelly... This way to the public conveniences...

I was so shocked when I saw my first Roman public loo. It's not that they're dirty. They're just way TOO public for me!

The public toilets near the Forum in Pompeii have twenty seats, and no cubicles. Don't be shy – this is another good place to listen in on people's conversations.

One of the oddest things about Roman toilets is what they have instead of toilet roll: in the public toilets you'll find a stick with a sponge on the end. After you've used it, please remember to rinse it off and leave it for the next person to use.

If you're a boy and you happen to need a pee as you're walking around Pompeii, you don't even have to find a toilet. Lots of people just go in the street, but it's more polite to look out for pots hanging on the wall. People who run laundries put them there and collect all the urine and use it for washing clothes.

Ewww! That's almost too disgusting even for me. Sorry I even mentioned it! Let's go and see what's going on in less stinky parts of the city.

Hear that? I can hear yelling. Bet I can guess what's going on in **here**...

I knew it. It's school time!
And someone's in trouble.

LATIN LESSONS

Plenty of kids in Roman times don't go to school at all. They just hang around with their parents and start learning the family trade as soon as they can walk and talk. And rich kids often get taught at home by a slave.

Some boys do get sent to school. If you're between six and eleven years old you could go to a school called the **ludus** to learn reading, writing and maths. Your teacher will probably be a Greek slave.

Even though they're slaves, you still have to do what your teachers say, and they'll beat you with an eel-skin strap if you get your sums wrong.

If you're going to go to school while you're in Pompeii, you should practise writing on a wax tablet. You use a pointy stick called a **stylus** instead of a pen to scratch words into the wax – and when you're finished, you rub them out with the blunt end and start again.

After eleven, some rich boys get sent to a grammaticus to learn more Latin and Greek, and after that if you show real promise you get sent to a teacher called a **rhetor** to learn...public speaking. Yes, this is the most valued skill of all for an important Roman.

It looks like playtime. Fancy a game, lads? I brought some old bones with me...

ASTRAGALI FOR BEGINNERS

Astragali may sound like the name of a master magician, but it's actually a pretty easy game. If you've ever played jacks, that's pretty much the same – only you can play this Roman version with bones from a goat's ankle.

1. Take five bones (or if you find that too icky, you can buy counters shaped like bones).
2. Throw them up in the air and catch as many as you can on the BACK of your hand.

3. If you don't manage to catch all five, pick up the ones you dropped with the same hand, without letting the others fall from the back of your hand.

4. See if your opponent can do any better!

Roman kids play some other games it's easy to join in with too, like leapfrog and hide and seek. Some of them even have some decent toys. Last time I was here I made friends with a boy who had his own chariot. He used to get a goat to pull him round town in it! I so wanted to take one of those home with me.

I don't know about you, but I reckon it must be lunchtime. If we keep going along here I know a great place to get a snack.

I think we'll be all right in this cafe, but there's some freaky food in Pompeii. We'll try to avoid bird brains.

71

LUNCH BREAK

In Pompeii, your diet depends on whether you're rich or poor. Poor people's food is very boring: mostly bread, with a bit of wheat porridge for a change. Other common foods you'll recognize are cottage cheese, honey, olives, and vegetables like cabbage, leeks and peas.

If you're looking for a snack, there are plenty of people selling food in the street. You could get a quick bowl of pea soup, a spicy meat pastry or a grilled sausage.

This is a **thermopolium**. It's a cross between a bar and a deli. Pick what you like the look of and then stand here and eat it. But be warned, there's something icky lurking in most of these pots...

This gloopy stuff's called 'garum' — it even sounds a bit like 'grim', doesn't it? It's a kind of fish sauce that's a speciality of Pompeii and you DON'T want to know how it's made. But let's find out anyway!

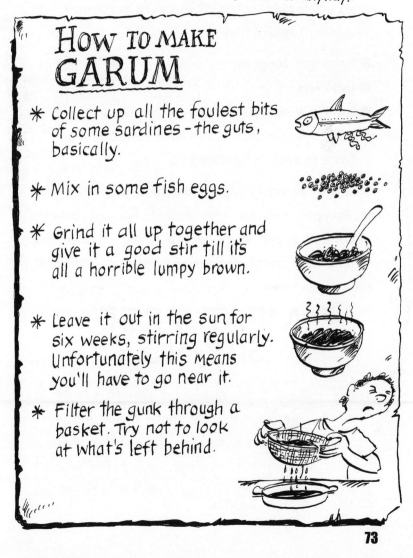

HOW TO MAKE GARUM

* Collect up all the foulest bits of some sardines – the guts, basically.

* Mix in some fish eggs.

* Grind it all up together and give it a good stir till it's all a horrible lumpy brown.

* Leave it out in the sun for six weeks, stirring regularly. Unfortunately this means you'll have to go near it.

* Filter the gunk through a basket. Try not to look at what's left behind.

Garum gets into everything. Romans just can't get enough of it. But that's not the strangest thing they eat. Rich people who can afford to will gobble up all kinds of horrible things. While you're in Pompeii, you should try some of these:

- flamingos' tongues
- fish livers
- sows' udders in tuna sauce
- bear (but take the doctor's advice and boil it up twice to avoid indigestion)

Believe it or not, there's some food you won't find in Pompeii because the ancient Romans haven't discovered it yet. So oranges, rice, sugar, coffee, tea, tomatoes, potatoes, peanuts and chocolate are all off the menu.

MEAT~FREE SPYING

Veggie History Spies should be able to survive in Pompeii – people don't eat much meat, and most people get by on bread, salad and cheese. It might be a problem avoiding that fish sauce. If you do find yourself at a posh dinner party and really can't bear to eat the roast boar which your host has generously laid on, you could just say that you're a vegetarian. There are some of them around – people who think that eating meat's cruel, that animals have souls, or even that eating meat makes you stupid and violent. You'll get some odd looks, but it's not unheard of.

DEADLY DISHES

Romans love the sweet taste that honey gives their food. But there's another way to make food sweet which has worse side effects than rotten teeth. Some cooks use lead pots and get that yummy sweet taste of poisonous lead into their dinner. Agents should avoid this as much as possible.

> Fancy a drink with your rotten-fish dinner? No lemonade, I'm afraid. Or orange juice. How about a nice cup of water?

Wine is the most popular drink for Ancient Romans, but it's usually diluted with water. You can also put honey in it if you don't like the taste, and you can buy hot wine if you're missing tea and coffee.

Milk isn't very common in cities. There's no refrigeration, so once milk has made it in from the countryside on a sunny Italian day it's often gone sour.

For a soft drink, try **posca**. It's mostly water, mixed with herbs and vinegar.

I spat my drink all over the place the first time I tried this stuff. Vinegar's good for chips but in a cup it's a bit of a shock!

That wasn't too bad, considering. I think we should go to see the main event round here – the games!

We should find some better clothes first. Just round this corner there should be... yes, here it is – a laundry. Handy how they hang their drying in the street, isn't it? Just keep a lookout while I borrow a couple of these smart tunics. OK, and now follow me quickly, in case anyone spots us.

TOUGH ON CRIME

The Romans have come up with some truly horrible things to do to people who break the law.

Some of them get sent to the silver mines in Spain, where you spend your whole time in dark tunnels and if you don't get buried alive you'll be worked to death. Criminals who've done something really bad, like murder, arson or treason, get a special punishment called **damnatio ad bestias** – being condemned to the beasts.

The whole town crowds into an amphitheatre to watch them get ripped apart by starved lions and bears.

We really, really musn't get caught doing anything illegal round here. You want to get home eventually, don't you?

Step Two in smartening up: we're off to have a bath. The Romans are obsessed with having baths, but they don't just mean lying in a tub with bubbles and a rubber duck.

BATHTIME

Whenever a mission takes you to Roman times, you should make sure to bathe regularly. Most Romans do. The baths aren't just places to get clean, they're gyms, cafes, libraries and general hangouts. And with all the businessmen and politicians having important meetings in the baths, you can find out all the latest gossip.

When you get to the baths, leave your clothes on the shelves in the changing room. Just next to the changing room is a **frigidarium** – this is a cold room, as you may have guessed from the name. You might want to jump into the pool in the middle once you've warmed up in the other parts of the baths.

FRIGIDARIUM

Oooh!

TEPIDARIUM

The **tepidarium** is the first room you'll go into. It's pretty warm, and there are benches where you can sit and get used to the heat.

Next is the **calidarium**, where things get really sweaty. It's the hottest room in the baths. You can sit and steam, wash yourself at the basin, or soak in the pool.

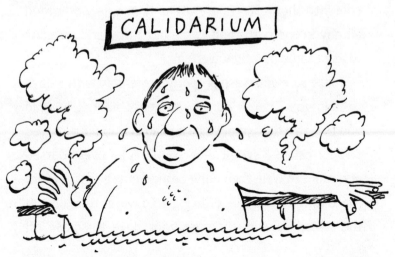

CALIDARIUM

You can still visit Roman baths in some parts of England.

In between the men's and women's hot rooms is a place called the **praefurnium** – a gap between the walls where you'll find furnaces, and slaves shovelling coal into them. Slaves are the only people who spend all day in the baths and come out filthy and smelling worse than when they went in.

Make sure you wash properly, preferably with a slave to help you. There's no shower gel or flannel. Instead you'll need a flask of olive oil and an evil-looking curved scraper called a **strigil**. Slop some oil all over yourself and rub it in well, then hang around in the steam room for as long as you like, drinking cold water to really get the sweat flowing. Then get your slave to scrape off all the oil, sweat and grime with the strigil. You'll be squeaky clean and ready to pose in the Forum with the best of them.

While you're at the baths, get your exercise fix in the outdoor courtyard. Your gym kit should be a short tunic, or a bikini if you're female. Try some wrestling, long jump, weightlifting (this one's popular with women) or playing with a hoop or a stick.

Look! A Roman bikini!

There's also a ball game you could join in with, called **trigon**, where the players stand in a triangle and throw the ball to each other. Or if you're not feeling so energetic, have a hot drink or buy a snack from a food vendor.

The baths are open every day from sunrise to sunset. Entry costs half an *as* for men, but at least one *as* for women. Kids get in for free.

I don't remember the last time I felt so clean. It's a weird feeling. Let's go and show it off, shall we? I've got tickets for the hottest show in town. We're going to the games!

Forget anything you might be thinking about the Olympics. The Roman games are all about violence, and it's not about 'taking part' – it's about 'not getting chopped to pieces'. This is the amphitheatre where it all happens, but there's nothing on today. We'll just do a quick trip back a couple of weeks with the annostat...

You can tell this is the only place to be. Just listen to that crowd! Let's find a good spot.

LADIES AND GENTLEMEN, PLEASE TAKE YOUR SEATS

The amphitheatre in Pompeii is famous. It's the oldest one in Italy and it seats 15,000 people. It's important to know your place – the seats are divided up for different classes of people, so go where you won't cause a scene.

The wooden seats nearest the front are for the very richest, most powerful men in Pompeii. Unless you have a very good disguise, you won't get in here.

The next seats up are for rich people as well. If you want a seat here, you'll have to look the part and be prepared to flash some cash.

The upper seats are for all the people who don't really count, like poor people or slaves.

Right up at the back, in the highest seats where you can't see so well, is a special area for rich ladies.

Other things to spot in the amphitheatre include:

- stalls along the walkways, selling tasty snacks and drinks
- attendants spraying perfumed water on to the crowd to cool them down
- the band: horns, trumpets and instruments called water organs provide the tunes to accompany the fighting
- the **lanista**: like a coach and a referee, this man can often be found at the edge of the ring yelling, 'Go on, kill him!'
- floggers: these people stand around the arena with whips and red hot irons, just in case anyone changes their mind and thinks they'd rather be somewhere else. Like back in bed.

Gladiator fights aren't always held in amphitheatres. Every now and again, an emperor will get over-excited and dig a whole new lake to have a real-life sea battle.

And in our time we just make do with war movies! When the Romans want to do something, they really go for it.

This is what an amphitheatre looks like from the outside.

Just like football supporters, fans of Roman gladiators are mad about their teams. Pompeii's had a major problem with hooligans in the past. Pompeii's big rivals are their neighbours in the town of Nuceria, but they don't just sing nasty songs about each other. In AD 59, at a gladiatorial fight, the fans from Pompeii and Nuceria were teasing each other as they always do. But then someone started throwing stones . . . and before you could say 'calm down' they were having a genuine battle where lots of people died. After that, they had to close the amphitheatre for ten years until everyone had agreed to play nicely.

WHERE THE WILD THINGS ARE

If you enjoy visits to the zoo, you might be interested to know that in a Roman amphitheatre you can see hippos, crocodiles, ostriches and rhinos. Sadly, you won't see any of them for very long. Romans love seeing exotic and scary animals, and then watching them being killed. Sometimes the animals are sent into the arena for a fight with a human. Often, there will be a big staged hunt where lots of animals can be killed at once. The organizers might place bushes all around the arena, so that it looks like the animals are being hunted in the wild.

Huge numbers of animals get caught around the Empire and hauled back to Italy for the games. Julius Caesar once had 600 lions, 400 other big cats and 20 elephants brought to be hunted in front of him. You can also watch fights between the animals themselves – maybe bear *v.* water buffalo, lion *v.* tiger, or bull *v.* rhino.

Animals are also used to kill prisoners – it's a handy way to punish criminals and entertain the crowd at the same time. The Romans are cruel, but they're quite inventive.

Hmm. Looks like we just missed the animal fights, but here come the stars of the show – the gladiators! Give them a cheer – everyone round here LOVES them. Some of these guys are more popular than the most famous footballers of our time.

GLADIATORS: A SPOTTER'S GUIDE

Gladiators wear impressive armour and have some terrifying weapons. But they don't just pick them out at random. There are several different types of gladiator, and rules about which type fights against which other type. Try to spot some of these when you're next at the games.

MURMILLO: he's armed with a short slashing sword, and he has a big rectangular shield and armour to repel any puny attacks you might try. Fights the Thracian, the Hoplomachus or the Retarius.

RETARIUS: the 'net man'. He'll catch you in his net and then stick you with a pointy trident or a short sword. Fights the Murmillo or the Secutor.

SECUTOR: like the Murmillo, he has a short sword – but this one's for stabbing people not slashing them open. He also has a rectangular shield, a brimless helmet, and arm guards.

THRACIAN: the popular favourite, the Thracian has a fabulously crested helmet, a short curved sword, a small square shield and armour on one arm and both legs. Fights the Hoplomachus mostly, or sometimes the Murmillo or another Thracian.

HOPLOMACHUS: has a straight sword, a spear and a small shield. His armour is almost the same as the Thracian's, but plainer. Fights the Murmillo or the Thracian.

They look amazing, don't they? I don't know though, I don't reckon it matters much whether your armour's shiny or not when you might be about to get killed. I don't think that's what would worry me. They're about to start...

IT'S A HARD- KNOCK LIFE

Gladiators don't usually sign up happily, thinking it sounds like an easy life. Don't forget that lots of them are criminals or slaves, and this is just one of the terrible things that might happen to you if you're caught committing a crime while on assignment in Roman times. Some are slaves who've annoyed their masters and have been sold to the gladiator schools. Some are free men who sign up hoping for some of the treasure and glory that successful gladiators get.

Agents who wish to train as gladiators should make sure they know when and where they can transport back to their own time without being seen. Leave it too late and you might have to fight, or be seen using your annostat and risk punishment from the Department for Historical Accuracy.

Once you've signed up as a gladiator, you go to gladiator training school where you'll learn to fight with wooden swords and wicker shields, so you can practise without damaging yourself beyond a few bruises and splinters. It takes a lot of hard training before you're fit enough to fight in front of a crowd. And it's not just fighting – you even have to learn the 'right' way to die. Remember: you stick your chest out, bow your head, and lean to the right as you fall. Obviously, you should try to avoid getting to this stage, but it's good to know what you should be practising.

In Pompeii, the gladiators live and train in the Theatre Quadriporticus. They're not chained up to stop them running away, and it can be a pretty good life if you survive. You get to waltz around in shiny armour with jewels and feathers, everybody loves you and you could even get rich.

SPORT THAT'S BAD FOR YOUR HEALTH

If you find beast hunts and gladiator fights just too horrible (and many History Spies do), you can still go and watch sport in Roman times. Be warned though – just because it's not the gladiators it doesn't mean there won't be blood.

CHARIOT RACES are very dangerous, and extremely popular. Even the horses who pull the chariots are celebrities. If a driver falls out and gets trampled to

This is what they might have looked like!

death during a race, as long as his horses keep on going and come in first then that chariot wins. Historians don't know exactly where races were held in Pompeii, so if you're on an assignment and disguised as a visitor from outside the city, please ask around and send a full report back to the Department.

BOXING MATCHES can often be seen in the Forum, sometimes to get the crowd warmed up before a day at the games. Roman boxers wear their hair in 'topknot' styles, and you can also spot them because of their gloves. But because they're fighting in front of Romans, they don't wear those namby-pamby padded gloves that boxers in the twenty-first century have. Instead, their gloves have balls of lead in the knuckles so it hurts more when they land a punch.

ATHLETICS is one sport the Romans like which doesn't usually end up with someone being carried off covered in blood. Of course, the Romans don't get quite as excited about it either. The Palaestra is a public space next to the amphitheatre where young men from the military society (Schola Juventutis) meet up to train, race, and generally show off their muscles.

You know what, I don't think I fancy any more 'sport'. It's very exciting but I reckon I may have had enough of that kind of excitement for now. Let's just head back to where we were in August. Here, just duck down this stairway while everyone's waiting for the next fight to start.
WHHHUMMMMMMMMMMMMMMMMMMMMMMMMMMMMMMMMMMMMMMMMMMMMMMMMMMMMMMMMMMMMM

A NIGHT AT THE ODEON

There are three theatres in this part of Pompeii, and the Odeon is the smallest. We could go there to hear some poetry, music, or public speaking in Latin, if you don't mind being bored to tears. I prefer the Odeons back in our time!

If you're going to the theatre in an Ancient Roman city, remember to take a picnic. Plays can go on for hours and hours. If you don't want a numb bum, don't forget your cushion.

The most popular plays are comedies and 'pantomimes' – but don't expect singalongs and people in cow costumes. A Roman pantomime is a play where the actors wear masks and mime a famous story.

Be as noisy as you like when you're at a Roman theatre. If you sit in silence people will think you're not enjoying yourself, or that you're just a grouch. If you are having a good time, there are different ways to show it, depending on how good you think it is.

HISSING: 'Rubbish, I want my money back.'

SNAPPING FINGERS: 'I'm mildly tickled.'

CLAPPING HANDS: 'This is great.'

WAVING A HANKY OR THE END OF YOUR TOGA: 'I LOVE it! Woo-hoo! Encore!'

Careful though – you might think that going to the theatre is a nice safe afternoon out compared to the gladiator fights with all the blood and guts. But in some Roman plays the actors get extra realism on the death scenes by killing a criminal live on stage. Check in advance that the play you're seeing doesn't involve a crucifixion or someone being burned alive. If you're lucky, you might see some acrobats and tightrope walkers.

Theatres and amphitheatres can have more uses for the History Spy than just relaxation and entertainment. If you suspect you're being followed, or if you've drawn attention to yourself by making a historical mistake, you can easily merge into the crowd here. There are plenty of entrances and exits, so once you're in it's easy to get out unnoticed.

ROMAN BOOK CLUB

Fancy a genuine Roman read? Try one of these.

THE SATYRICON by Petronius. This is a comedy about people in the towns around Pompeii. It features a crazy dinner party given by an ex-slave with plenty of money but no idea how to behave.

THE AENEID by Virgil. Virgil's the greatest Roman poet and the Aeneid is a real epic adventure, all about the Trojan wars.

THE ART OF LOVE by Ovid. Before dating websites and agony aunts, the Romans had Ovid.

The problem is, you can't exactly curl up with a book in Pompeii. For starters, there's no such thing as a book. They're written on papyrus scrolls which can be up to eight metres long, and you need a slave to help you unroll your scroll. Even if you could manage, papyrus breaks a lot more easily than paper. If you fell asleep while reading in bed, you'd wake up in a huge heap of papyrus crumbs.

This graffiti's a bit weird. It doesn't really say anything. Hang on, I think it's a code! It might be a mission for us. Help me work it out, will you?

IVHTEGDERILSSAFEVAFMORMURO

Hmm... I can see 'safe' and, er, 'deril'. Nope, that can't be right. Let me just leaf through the code book for a sec. Maybe this is the bit we want...

SECRET MESSAGES

The Romans know a couple of simple ways to hide messages before they send them. You can hide the words, maybe by writing them inside a shallow wooden box that becomes a normal wax tablet (see page 68) when you pour wax in it. An innocent message can be written in the wax when it sets. The person who wants to read the secret message just melts the wax and pours it out. Or you could do the same with a person. Take a slave, shave off his hair, tattoo your message on the back of his head, and then wait for the hair to grow back and cover up the writing. Obviously this method does take time so it's not so good for urgent messages.

The Roman leader Julius Caesar himself has given his name to a simple code called the 'Caesar cipher'. Write out the alphabet and then each time you want to use a letter, count along three places and use that letter instead. To decode a message, you just write out the alphabet and

count backwards three places. Try this method
to read the following message:

FKDUOLH ZRC HUH

— — — — — — — — — — — —

To make your messages extra safe, History Spies
should use better codes than this. If you use a
code the Romans know about, they're more likely
to be able to read your messages.

WRITING BY NUMBERS

If you can see a number at the start of a coded
message, it's sometimes a clue that the message
has been split into blocks. To unscramble the
words, first cross the number off the beginning
of the message (but remember what it was).
Next, split up the message into blocks, each one
containing the number of letters that you got
from the number at the start. It will still look
like gobbledegook. But turn each of the blocks
backwards and all should be clear.

For instance, **5ERCESTSIHTPSYROEDOCY** turns into this:

ERCES TSIHT PSYRO EDOCY

and when you turn each block backwards, it should unscramble as **SECRET HISTORY SPY CODE**.

Remember, Romans don't use our numbers, so you'll need to look out for Roman numerals at the start of the message instead. If you need help with Roman numbers, remember the guide on pp. 25–6.

IVHTEGDERILSSAFEVAFMORMURO

- -

Well? What do you make it?

Answer: Get hired as slave from Forum

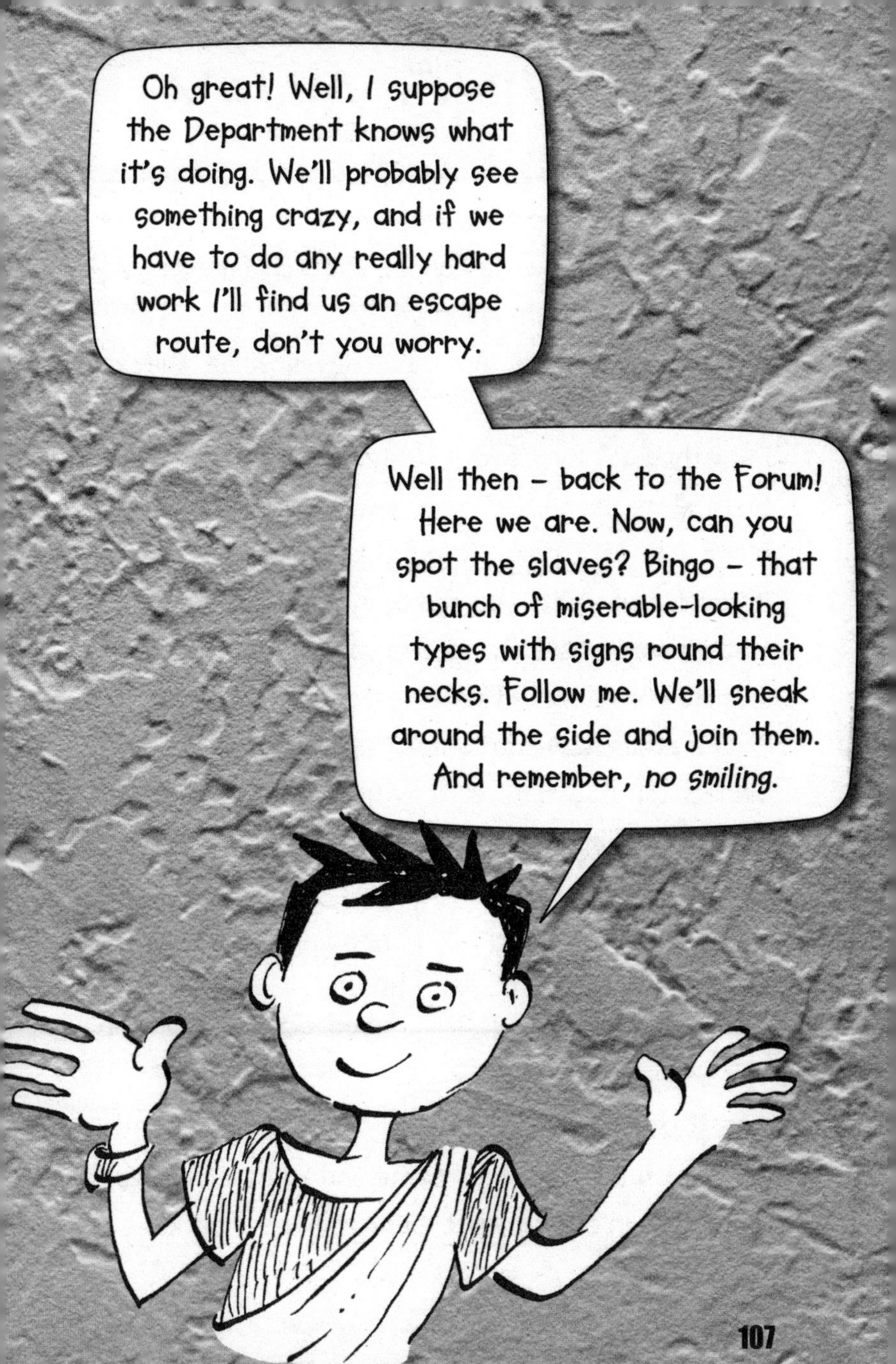
Oh great! Well, I suppose the Department knows what it's doing. We'll probably see something crazy, and if we have to do any really hard work I'll find us an escape route, don't you worry.
Well then – back to the Forum! Here we are. Now, can you spot the slaves? Bingo – that bunch of miserable-looking types with signs round their necks. Follow me. We'll sneak around the side and join them. And remember, *no smiling*.

SLAVING AWAY

Slaves do *everything* in the Roman Empire. About a third of all the people in the Empire are slaves. Even ordinary people own a couple, and rich families can afford to keep several hundred.

The Romans pick up their slaves while they're abroad fighting wars. When they take prisoners, they bring these captives back to Italy where they can make themselves useful. But you could also find yourself being sold as a slave if you're kidnapped by pirates, if you run up debts you can't pay, or if you're a child whose parents have abandoned you. And some unlucky kids are born slaves, like their parents.

Once these slaves in Pompeii have been bought, their owners can do whatever they like with them. They'll have to fetch and carry for their masters, and do everything their masters can't be bothered to do for themselves.

> Oh no – so we could be heading for a week of tidying up someone else's bedroom. How unfair would that be?

Some people make their slaves wear tags around their necks with their master's name and address on them, like people in our time put round their pets' necks.

Agents must be very careful if they're ordered to work undercover disguised as slaves. Trying to escape is an extremely serious offence, and you risk having the letters FUG burned on to the skin of your forehead with a red hot iron if you're caught. FUG is short for 'fugitivus', which is Latin for 'runaway'. Your master also has the right to beat you or even kill you, and no one can say anything about it.

But these slaves actually don't have much to moan about. They've been chosen to work in a city because they're the young, clever, pretty ones. The unlucky reject slaves get sent to farms or even worse, down the mines. Down there they get chained up in the dark and worked until they drop. Most of the slaves you see around here will be freed before they get old. If a slave works hard and stays on the right side of his boss, he can be freed and start a new life on his own.

If you're trying to pass as a slave, you need to look the part. For an auction, you'll have a sign round your neck giving details like your age, where you're from,

and whether you've got any defects or a history of disobedience. If your Latin's not perfect yet, whiten the soles of your feet with chalk. That's a sign that you've only just been brought in from abroad.

There's more to looking like a slave than just wearing a sign, though. Once you've been a slave for a while you'll really start to look different from your masters. Because Roman slaves do all the work and don't get the good food, they're shorter than the rich people and bent out of shape, with bad teeth and creaky bones. They can look like a totally different species – which is also how they get treated.

HOME SWEET HOME

This is a typical house belonging to a rich family in Pompeii. There are lots of rooms: in the middle of the first set of rooms you come to, you'll see a little indoor pool. When it rains, the water fills up the pool and then the family can use it.

All the nice houses in Pompeii are decorated with mosaics and have brightly painted walls. No Pompeii gentleman would be happy to have his walls just one boring colour. Instead, the walls have pictures on them, sometimes of well-known stories and sometimes of fake columns. You'll even see fake doors painted in rooms, standing open and looking out on to gardens. Remember not to try to walk through any of these by accident or you'll get a sore nose *and* look stupid.

Even though this house is one of the fanciest around, there are hardly any windows. There isn't much glass available here yet, so you'll only see some little high-up windows with bars on them.

I guess that's why they paint fake views on their walls. You could pretend you lived anywhere if it wasn't for all the noise outside.

In summer, these houses are nice and cool, but in winter it gets dark and smoky with the fires burning inside the house to keep it warm. After dark, people light their houses with olive oil lamps. They're expensive and smoky, and don't give much light. That, and the fact that spectacles haven't been invented yet, means that lots of people over thirty can't see to read. They have to get slaves to read for them.

None of the houses in Pompeii have very much furniture. Romans mostly make do with a few stools and couches.

I think this is a brilliant idea. When I grow up I'm just going to have beds in every room instead of chairs and sofas and boring stuff like that. And I'm going to eat all my meals in bed, just like the Romans do.

PARTY ANIMALS

Rich Romans love to have dinner parties. It's their favourite way to relax in the evening. They also use dinner parties to butter up their VIP friends and to show off how rich and sophisticated they are.

History Spies always find dinner parties interesting and useful, as well as fun. This is where you'll really get to know the people who run Pompeii. Look out for a rose hanging from the ceiling. The old story goes that Cupid gave a rose to the god of silence to stop him blabbing about all the goddess Aphrodite's secret boyfriends. So now, anything that's said 'under the rose' has to stay a secret outside that room. And that means that a lot of secrets get shared at dinner parties. Whether you get invited as a guest or have to offer your services as a slave, all History Spies should try to go to a dinner party while they're in Pompeii.

> Sounds like fun... for the people who get to eat all the food! Still, remembering all that Roman food we heard about before, I'm not sure I could manage to eat it without choking.

DISGUSTING DELICACIES

Some of the food you'll see at posh dinners in Pompeii will turn your stomach. Some of it will confuse you. But if it looks like something you wouldn't normally touch, don't be put off. Round here, nothing is what it seems, and disguised food is all the rage.

Roast dormice stuffed with minced pork, pepper, pine kernels and garum

Peas mixed with grains of real gold

Ostrich brains

Custard made o calves' brains and rosehips

I think this must be the dormouse jar! Put your ear against it – you can hear them scrabbling around.

They keep them in the dark because that makes them want to eat all the time. With all those nuts in there with them, the dormice get tasty and fat really quickly. Fancy one?

BE THE PERFECT DINNER GUEST

If you're lucky enough to be invited to a dinner when you're on an assignment in Pompeii, you'll need to know what to expect.

First, dress for dinner. Look stylish and elegant without the discomfort of a toga – wear a **synthesis**. In this cross between a toga and a tunic, you can lounge around, stretch across the table, and really let your hair down without worrying about whether your toga's about to unravel around you.

MIND YOUR MANNERS

DON'T:	DO:
✗ argue	✓ lounge around
✗ swear	✓ spit
✗ sit down	✓ burp
	✓ eat till you're sick

When you get to the dining room, you'll find three couples arranged like this:

Make sure you wait to find out exactly where your place is. There's normally space for three guests on each couch, and the place you're given shows exactly where you fit in order of importance. But remember, only foreigners and country bumpkins sit at the table to eat. Civilized people lie down. First, get a slave to take off your shoes and wash your feet for you. Also wash your hands – a slave will provide a bowl of water. Then lie down, leaning on your left elbow and using your right hand to eat and drink.

The Romans don't have forks, and you won't see any knives at a fancy banquet either. All the food will be already cut into bits for you. Just use your fingers, and a spoon for the sauce. Toothpicks will be provided.

They're eating out in the garden, apparently. Here, carry this – er – pile of brains, and follow me.

WANTED: WAITERS – MUST HAVE GOOD BEDSIDE MANNER

If you're undercover as a slave, working at a dinner party is a perfect spying opportunity. But you must get your job absolutely right. Your master is hoping to make a great impression on his guests and he won't stand for slaves who are clumsy with the soup.

There's a lot of preparation to be done before a party. Number one on the slave's to-do list: the shopping. Head to the Forum to get your meat, fish and exotic imported treats: honey from Greece, olive oil from Africa, grain from Britain, and spices from the East. You might be sent on some ridiculous errands. One story about a Roman emperor called Heliogabalus (who hasn't been born yet) says that he poured so many sweet-smelling flowers from the ceiling on to his dinner guests that some of them suffocated to death. Imagine how much work the slaves had to do to set *that* up. There's less exciting work to do too – the cook will need you to carry lots of water and firewood into the kitchen.

Once the guests arrive, it's one particular slave's job

to call them names. Actually, that should be 'call out their names'. He's the nomenclator, or 'name-caller', who announces each person as they enter. Other slaves should wash the guests' hands and feet.

Then the dishes should be brought out from the kitchen and put on the table in the middle of the three

dining couches, so everyone can reach them. Sometimes there might be a pool of water instead of a table, with each dish floating on a mini model of a boat or bird. There will also be music during or after the meal. History Spies who play the guitar could practise a stringed instrument called the lyre, or if you play the recorder you could try a set of pipes called the **tibiae**. If you're a skilled dancer, or if you think you're funny and want to try your hand at being a clown, you could be the after-dinner entertainment.

Once you've waited for the last drunken guest to finally roll home, you're all done. Apart from the clearing up.

What? I'm not sticking around for that. Anyway, we don't want to stay for the end when all the slaves get sent back to the guy who hired us out. We'd better get out of here while everyone's busy – they won't miss us.

We should get right out of town to make sure there's no trouble. We'll have to sneak through the gate...

> ... and now here we are, in the CITY OF THE DEAD! Whoooooo! It's pretty spooky, but it's much less scary than being caught as a runaway slave.

DEAD END STREET

You are now entering the Necropolis. It's a Greek word, and it means 'City of the Dead'. Romans don't shut tombs away in walled-off cemeteries. They build them along the main roads out of town, and you'll find stalls in between the graves selling snacks and trinkets. The tombs themselves can be quite grand, and on some of them you'll see pipes sticking out. This is so people can pour some wine down to their great-grannies to keep them happy. Romans think the spirits of the dead get

angry a lot, and they'll keep haunting the living if they don't make an effort to cheer them up.

When a Roman dies, they're usually cremated amongst the tombs, wearing their best clothes. If an important person dies while you're in Pompeii, you'll see a big funeral procession called a **pompa**. The family will hire mourners to weep and wail dramatically. There will also be musicians, slaves to carry the body, and actors wearing wax masks to make them look like the dead person's other important ancestors. You might even be treated to some stand-up comedy from a clown who makes jokes about the dead person.

> No wonder they think the spirits are angry! I'd be pretty cross if people were taking the mickey at my funeral.

AVOIDING DEATH

There are several unpleasant diseases that could strike you down while you're in Pompeii. Make sure you're vaccinated against common diseases like tuberculosis and typhoid before you go. Malaria is a big killer – it causes a nasty fever with flu-like symptoms, and can lead to a coma and death. It's passed on by mosquitoes, though the Romans don't know this yet. Stay one step ahead by wearing mosquito repellent.

You should also take diarrhoea remedies with you, or learn to mix up the right amount of salt, sugar and water to drink. Otherwise you can easily get dehydrated and die. You can avoid diarrhoea and worse diseases like cholera by making sure you drink clean water – always boil it. It's also a good idea not to use the shared sponges in the toilets, because of all the germs. *Yeah – like we needed telling!*

There is good news too – some diseases haven't made it to Europe yet, like smallpox. The Roman army will bring that back with them from Persia in AD 165. Thanks, lads.

BAD MEDICINE

If you start to feel ill, transport back to your own time immediately if you think it might be serious. If you need surgery, you definitely don't want to hang around in Roman times. There's at least one surgeon in Pompeii – archaeologists have found some of his tools. But however skilled he is, it's still going to hurt, and the only painkiller the Romans have is poppy juice.

If you have a minor complaint and want to try out Roman medicine, you might be surprised by the diagnosis. Roman doctors think that everyone has

four disgusting-sounding 'humours' inside them: blood, phlegm, black bile and yellow bile. Any disease must mean your humours are unbalanced. So doctors will try all sorts of unpleasant things to balance them up again. They'll bleed you, pump medicine up your bottom, or make you vomit. It's enough to make you lose your sense of humour completely. Ask for some medicine, and you'll get a familiar bad taste – it's that rotten-fish garum again. They prescribe it for dog bites, diarrhoea, ulcers and everything in between.

Perhaps you don't feel like going to the doctor's any more? You could always try praying to Aesculapius, the god of medicine. Get a little model of the part of your body that's giving you trouble, and leave it in Aesculapius's temple when you make a sacrifice there. You could also have a nap while you're in the temple. If you sleep there all night you might have a healing dream where the god appears and cures you.

One doctor who would be useful in Pompeii is a decent dentist. Everybody has bad teeth. Rich people have rotten teeth from eating too many sweet things, and poor people grind their teeth away on the rough bread which is all they get to eat. You'll have to get used to the smell of bad breath if you stay in Pompeii for long.

DISASTER STRIKES

Before AD 79, the Romans don't realize Mount Vesuvius is dangerous. They think it's a great place to grow olives and grapevines. They're right – but the reason the soil on Vesuvius is so good for farming is that it came from inside the mountain long ago. This means it's full of minerals like iron, chalk and sulphur. For hundreds of years, the people of Pompeii have been cheerfully living just six miles away from an angry volcano.

Today, on 24 August AD 79, Vesuvius is going to blow. More than 2,000 people in Pompeii will die in the next two days.

History Spies should on no account stay in Pompeii during the eruption to see what happens. It's far too dangerous. But archaeologists have worked out the story of the disaster from what they've dug up –layers of ash, smashed buildings, and the bodies of people who died while they were trying to escape. Don't get caught yourself. Go to a safe place at least ten miles away from Vesuvius, for instance Misenum – or even better, get back to your own time.

What do you think? We could go back to our own time. We've completed our mission and got plenty of good information. But seeing as it's your first time here in Pompeii, I vote we stay and watch the eruption. You've never seen anything like it before, I promise!
Aha, the perfect getaway boat! This one's taking wine and oil over to the naval base at Misenum. Now we just have to get on board quietly, without being seen, and hide down in the hold. I hope you don't get seasick.

FRONT~ROW SEATS

Misenum is a base for the Roman navy. It's a few miles across the Bay of Naples from Pompeii, so it's a safe distance from Vesuvius – but when the volcano erupts, there's an amazing view from there.

You see those two people over there? The man and the boy? They're both called Pliny, and they're about to get really important. It's all thanks to those guys that historians know so much about what happens when Vesuvius erupts.

The grown-up Pliny is the commander of the navy here at Misenum. He's also a historian and a scientist in his spare time. And the young Pliny is his seventeen-year-old nephew, who's staying with his uncle. They've both got a rough couple of days ahead of them.

ALL SHOOK UP

For a few days, earth tremors have been shaking the ground around Vesuvius. Some people have already packed up and left town. But the ground often shakes around here, so not everyone thinks it's an emergency.

MIDDAY: BOOM!

At about 12 p.m. there's a huge bellowing noise as the mountain splits open. Then an enormous mushroom-shaped cloud shoots out of the volcano, blocking out the sunlight and turning the sky black. Now people really start to panic.

In Misenum, Pliny the Elder sees the cloud and orders his men to get a boat ready so that he can go and take a closer look. As a scientist, he can't wait to see a volcano in action. But just then, he gets a note from his friend who lives near Vesuvius asking Pliny for help – so he heads off on a rescue mission instead.

Pliny the Younger isn't taking any chances – he stays behind in Misenum with his mum to do his homework.

Lucky he was such a geek...

137

LUNCHTIME:
HERE COMES THE RAIN

As the ash cloud moves over Pompeii, hot ash and tiny pebbles start to rain down on the towns around the mountain. This rain will carry on all afternoon, through the night to the next morning. You can still move around the streets if you tie a cushion to your head to protect you from hot flying rocks. But as the piles of ash build up, the streets get harder to walk through. Some people decide to stay indoors until it's all over – but all that ash is heavy, and it's starting to make roofs fall in and buildings collapse. The earth's still shaking too.

LATER THAT NIGHT:
THE PLINYS GET NERVOUS

Over in Misenum, Pliny the Younger and his mum get out of the house because it's wobbling all over the place. In the early morning they head down to the seashore, but things don't look good there either. The sea has rushed away from the town after the sea floor was shaken by the eruption, leaving fish stranded all over the beach.

Things are even worse for Pliny's uncle. Pliny the Elder makes it to his friend's house in Stabiae, and can't go any further. To keep everyone else calm he acts as if he's not worried, and gets a good night's sleep.

Eventually the building's shaking so much, and there's so much ash falling, that Pliny and his friend also head for the beach. But the dust and gases in the air are thick and Pliny's old lungs can't cope. He collapses on the beach, with two slaves trying to help him, and he's found dead the next day.

THE NEXT MORNING: THINGS GET EVEN WORSE...

Early in the morning, the 'rain' stops. But there's worse to come. Suddenly, a load of hot ash and gas comes rushing down the mountain at terrifying speed. This happens several times, and after a few hours a surge gets to Pompeii. Anyone who's still left alive in the city will be instantly frazzled.

Any minute now, there's a surge headed right for Misenum.

Seriously, it's time we got out of here before we're toast. Burned, dusty toast.

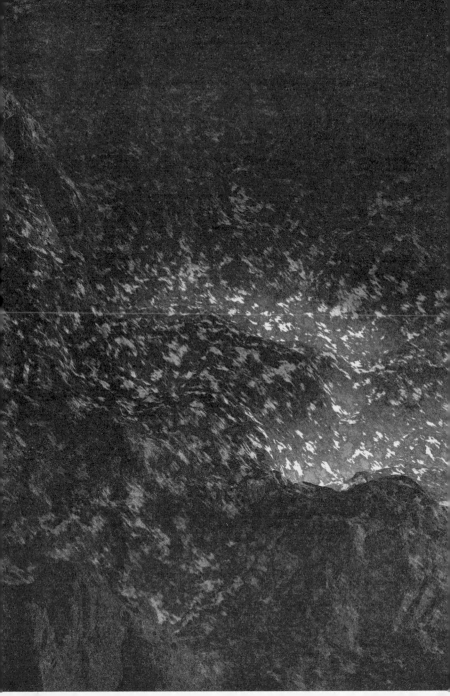

There's not going to be much to do around here now anyway. Pompeii's gone, and it won't be found again for almost 1,700 years. Put your finger on the annostat again...
WHHHUMM

You can go to Pompeii again these days. They've dug up a lot of it, and you can walk around all the same streets and everything. It's not as good without all the slaves and gladiators and crazy gods. Still, nowadays you can get pizza and ice cream instead of just fishy brains, so it's not all bad.

Oh, and just so you know – Pliny the Younger was fine. He survived the disaster and wrote about it later. Looks like staying behind to do his homework saved his life! My teachers would love that story.

Thanks for coming along – that was definitely a successful History Spy mission. Just let me know if you want to go back some time, or if there's somewhere else you'd like to try out for spying adventures. See you!

TIME MAP

Use this guide to make sure you don't drop into the 'wrong' bit of the Roman Empire. Avoid fatal mistakes like being Christian in the wrong year, or arriving in Pompeii after the volcano erupts.

753 BC
Legend says the city of Rome was founded by a boy called Romulus.

264 BC
First record of a gladiator fight.

250 BC
By now the Romans have conquered most of Italy.

218 BC
Hannibal the Carthaginian brings thirty-seven elephants (and 35,000 men) over the Alps to attack Rome.

200 BC
Romans start using concrete for buildings.

73 BC
Spartacus leads a slave revolt in southern Italy – his men hide in a crater of Vesuvius.

55 BC
Julius Caesar invades Britain – but doesn't quite finish the job.

49 BC	Julius Caesar marches into Rome and becomes its dictator.
44 BC	Caesar is murdered by a group led by Brutus.
30 BC	Egypt becomes a Roman province.
27 BC	Julius Caesar's adopted son Octavius becomes first Roman emperor and takes the name Augustus.
AD 30	Jesus crucified in the Roman province of Judaea.
AD 42	Claudius invades Britain.
AD 50	Roman traders reach Bengal and India.
AD 59	A fight at a gladiator game in Pompeii turns into a battle with the neighbours from Nuceria.
AD 60	Boudicca leads a revolt against the Romans in Britain.

An earthquake rocks Pompeii and destroys lots of buildings – people soon get rebuilding.	**AD 62**
A huge fire rips through the city of Rome. Some people say the Emperor started it!	**AD 64**
Small earth tremors shake Pompeii again – but no one picks up on the fact that it's a sign the volcano is ready to blow.	**AD 70**
VESUVIUS ERUPTS – Pompeii is buried under layers of ash!	**AD 79**
Completion of the Colosseum.	**AD 80**
The Empire reaches its biggest size under Emperor Trajan.	**AD 117**
Plague spreads through the Empire.	**AD 165–7**
The Empire is divided into East and West.	**AD 395**

AD 476 Western Empire falls.

AD 1453 Eastern Empire falls.

AD 1592 Workers digging a canal uncover part of Pompeii – and then cover it up again.

AD 1748 Archaeologists start work on digging up a city near Vesuvius, but they don't know which one it is yet.

AD 1763 Archaeologists stumble across an inscription that proves they're digging up the ancient town of Pompeii.

Back to the Blitz

TIME SPIES

Have you ever been on a top-secret, life-and-death, time-bending government mission before?

Liverpool: 1940

The war is raging and the Department of Historical Accuracy need a brave and daring History Spy to uncover the truth...

Your mission: learn how to identify enemy aircraft, make spitfires out of saucepans and disguise yourself as an evacuee. Find out how people spoke, what they ate, and become a champion at marbles!

Join top History Spy Charlie Cartwright in his adventures as he travels through space and time, dodging bombs, dinosaurs and erupting volcanoes.

TONY ROBINSON

The Worst Children's Jobs in History

Your paper round will never seem so bad again!

The Worst Children's Jobs in History takes you back to a time when being a kid was no excuse. Tony Robinson takes you on a guided tour through all the lousiest places for a kid to work, and tells you all the most back-breaking, puke-inducing bits of being a child in the past!

A selected list of titles available from Macmillan Children's Books

The prices shown below are correct at the time of going to press. However, Macmillan Publishers reserves the right to show new retail prices on covers, which may differ from those previously advertised.

History Spies: Escape from Vesuvius Jo Foster	978-0-330-44900-7	£4.99
History Spies: The Great Exhibition Mission Jo Foster	978-0-330-44901-4	£4.99
History Spies: Search for the Sphinx Jo Foster	978-0-330-44903-8	£4.99
History Spies: Back To The Blitz Jo Foster	978-0-330-44899-4	£4.99
The Worst Children's Jobs in History Tony Robinson	978-0-330-44286-2	£6.99
How Loud Can You Burp? Glenn Murphy	978-0-330-45409-4	£5.99
Stuff That Scares Your Pants Off! Glenn Murphy	978-0-330-47724-6	£4.99
The Ultimate Survival Guide Mike Flynn	978-0-230-70051-2	£9.99

All Pan Macmillan titles can be ordered from our website, www.panmacmillan.com, or from your local bookshop and are also available by post from:

Bookpost, PO Box 29, Douglas, Isle of Man IM99 1BQ

Credit cards accepted. For details:
Telephone: 01624 677237
Fax: 01624 670923
Email: bookshop@enterprise.net
www.bookpost.co.uk

Free postage and packing in the United Kingdom